How To Be Happy

Find Happiness in Your Life with Simple Strategies

Shalu Sharma

Other books by the author

Self discovery books

Self Discovery Journal: 121 Thought Provoking Questions:
Journal Questions for Women
Journal for Girls: 101 Thought Provoking Question: Journal
Questions for Girls
Journal for Women: 105 Questions for Women with
Motivational Quotes: Self Discovery Journal
Gratitude Journal: Keep a Gratitude Journal and Turn Pain to
Joy

Books on religion

An Introduction to the Way of the Buddha: Buddhism for
Beginners
Buddhist Teachings, Beliefs, Finding Enlightenment and
Practicing Buddhism
Hinduism for Beginners

Table of contents

Why are people unhappy

Have you ever asked yourself why so many people are unhappy? There has truly never been a better time in human history to be alive, and yet people are still unhappy and depressed all over the place. We're not just talking about people in developing countries either. Even people in rich countries, such as the United States and the United Kingdom, have high rates of depression and suicide. The reason for this may very well have to do with technology and all the choices in life available to us. Human beings are actually very simple creatures who like to make easy choices without much complexity to them. If you had too many choices then it causes stress and anxiety, even if they are superficial choices. For example, women are known for having lots of different shoes and outfits in their closet. Having to decide over which shoes and outfit to wear can cause stress. The same goes for having too many choices of foods in the supermarket, places to travel, or even houses to purchase. People who have more money tend to be the ones who have more choices like this. This is where the old saying "money doesn't buy happiness" comes from. It has to do with people having money to purchase anything they want and not knowing what to purchase because there are just too many choices. This makes them miserable and actually causes them to have suicidal tendencies over it.

Now let's look at unhappiness from a broader scale. No matter if you are rich or poor, chances are you use Facebook if you have an internet connection. Facebook is the most powerful social media network in the world and has over one billion registered users. People from all walks of life spend hours each day checking their Facebook accounts and seeing what their friends are up to. However, this doesn't really make them happy because they aren't seeing their friends in person.

All they are doing is looking at status updates on their friends and seeing pictures of their lives without actually being physical with them. This can cause a person to feel isolated and depressed because they aren't having the kind of fun and excitement that their friends are having. Instead, they live vicariously through them on Facebook which leads to great unhappiness. You will become the type of person who has a wandering mind and lives in their imagination to find happiness rather than finding it in real life. So when you end up having to come out of your imagination and face your life, it will make you very unhappy.

One particular area that makes most people unhappy is work. About 90% of the people in this world do not like the job they work at. The reason for this doesn't have so much to do with the work itself, but rather their lack of control at work. What irritates employees more than anything is having a boss who is unfair and gives them a heavy workload without additional compensation. No one likes to be treated unfairly and it will only add to your unhappiness and depression. As a result, you may end up eating junk food to try and give yourself a quick fix of happiness. But eating junk food will ultimately lead to additional unhappiness in the long run. Studies have shown that people who eat pizza, hamburgers, and other commercial fast food are more prone to developing depression. Unhappiness can become much worse like this over time if you continue to make bad choices like these.

Meditation for Stress Relief

Meditation is one of the oldest mental practices for relieving stress. Hindus and Buddhists have used meditation for thousands of years to center themselves and have mental clarity. But the great thing about meditation is you don't need to be associated with any religion to do it. All you need to know are the basic steps in performing meditation and what you can expect from it. Meditation is all about relaxing the body so that you feel no stress. As a result, you will have a reduced heart rate, low blood pressure, relaxed muscles, and peace of mind. The way you perform meditation is by taking your mind off the negative thoughts and feelings you are experiencing. For most people, this would mean sitting in front of the television and being distracted by their favorite show to ease their mind. But studies have shown that television and movies actually do very little to fight stress. In fact, it could make it worse if the images you see on television disturb you or remind you of whatever is making you angry. The only way to fight stress is to allow the body to heal itself naturally.

Meditation involves sitting in a calm environment, breathing slow and deeply, and thinking of one thing that brings you happiness. You can close your eyes when you do this if it will help keep your environment from distracting you. However, a lot of people like to use a picture of their family or some visual aid during meditation in order to stay focused more easily. If you are new to meditation then you may find this helpful. On the other hand, if you are able to close your eyes and just visualize a happy thought in your head then that will work just the same. As long as you are in an environment that is quiet and peaceful, you will have everything you need to start meditation. It should be performed for at least 20 minutes per day just like physical exercise. Most people like to meditate in the morning after they just wake up because it motivates them and helps them start the day properly. But if you have more time to spare then you should meditate three times per day; once in the morning, once in the afternoon, and once in the evening. That way you relieve your stress gradually throughout the course of the day before it starts to build up again.

There are different types of meditation exercises that put more emphasis on certain aspects of regular meditation. Deep breathing meditation, for example, is where you mentally focus on each deep breath that you make and nothing else. You must breathe in through your nose and out through your mouth to get the best sense of relaxation from this. Hum meditation is another type of meditation where you actually hum a name or word repeatedly that gives you happiness. This could be the name of your god, the name of your family member or an object that you like. Some people even say the word "hum" because it is a soothing word to them. Whatever works for you is fine. But the one meditation that is commonly practiced all over the world is yoga meditation. Yoga is a discipline that enhances your spiritual, physical and mental wellbeing. Yoga exercises involve positioning your body in peculiar positions while in a meditative state. It is a more advanced form of meditation but it is found to be very effective for relaxing your body and mind together. But no matter which type of meditation you choose for yourself, just stick with it and you will notice a change in your happiness very quickly.

Expressing gratitude to be happy

As human beings, it is easy for us to take what we have in life for granted. How often do you say "thank you" to someone who has done something nice for you? Better yet, how often do you appreciate the opportunities you've had in life and the people you've been fortunate to have in it? Most people never express their gratitude for all that they have. Instead, they dwell upon the things they don't have in their life such as a million dollars and a beachfront house in Hawaii. Yes, these would be nice things to have in life but they are not everything. There are people in this world who have it so much worse than you do. Finding happiness can be achieved if you value what is important in life rather than what is not important.

Think about the Syrian refugees who are escaping their war-torn country just to find sanctuary somewhere else. They could only dream about having all of the advantages and opportunities you've had in life, and yet you probably take them for granted and still complain about the things you don't have. If this is what you do then it is no wonder why you are not happy. Therefore, if you want to be happier then try to show gratitude for everything you do have. This means thanking people more often and feeling good overall about the positive things you have in your life. Try feeling grateful that you have a job, money, house, food, and friends to talk with. Many people in this world don't have any of these things. Once you realize this, it is much easier to feel happier in your life.

Expressing gratitude may be a difficult thing for you to do at first. You may be such a bitter and unhappy person that you don't want to thank anybody for anything, even if they rightfully deserve it. But try not to think so much about why you are doing it. Sometimes happiness can originate from the actions you perform rather than the thoughts you have in your head. Being kind and grateful towards other people will make them like you more and want to be friendly with you. This will make you have a higher opinion of people and they will have a higher opinion of you. As a result, you'll have more self-esteem and feeling of self-worth than you ever had before. These two elements are the true keys to happiness and they are pretty easy to obtain if you can change your perspective on life.

Studies have proven that people who are ungrateful tend to be more materialistic. If you are the type of person who cares more about possessions and money rather than human beings then chances are you're unhappy inside. Rather than thinking that more possessions will make you happier, try helping others with the money and power that you have. The idea of expressing gratitude in order to be happy isn't just a verbal thing. You need to show others how grateful you are for the things you have in your life by helping others out who are more unfortunate than you are. This will not only make you feel more grateful that you are not like them, but it will help them feel more grateful to have somebody like you who is giving them a helping hand. This will, in turn, make you feel even happier that you were able to do this for them. Then others will respect and admire you more. Isn't that what we all want in order to be happy?

Exercise for happiness

Sometimes the key to happiness is more physical than it is mental. A big reason why so many people are unhappy in the modern world is because they don't move around as much anymore. Most people use automobiles when they travel away from their home. Not only that, but many of the newest jobs require people to sit down rather than move around. When you think about all the sitting that people do in a given day, it is no wonder why they are depressed. Human beings are supposed to move around more than we are meant to sit down. This doesn't mean you have to do high-intensity exercises like running or swimming, it just means walking instead of sitting. By incorporating walking into your life, it will make you much happier as a result. But if you were to take it a step further and actually perform exercises then it would make you even more happier.

I always go for long walks. Nature walks are the best.

The reason why exercise makes you happier is because the brain's pituitary gland releases neurotransmitters called "endorphins" anytime the body is put under strenuous exercise or stress. These endorphins target the central nervous system in order to help you ease your stress and help you relax. As a result, you will be happy instead of sad. This is just the scientific reason why exercise makes you happier. Exercise can also make you happy when you are performing it outside or with other people. For example, you could jog for 30 minutes on a treadmill each day and feel a little happier because of it. But if you were to jog outside around your block for 30 minutes each day then you may feel even happier. There is a physiological effect that nature has on our minds which can put us at ease. All of the elements of nature play a part in this such as the sun, wind, grass, trees and so on. When you're around these elements it'll make you feel alive and free rather than being cooped up in a house or gym and feeling isolated. Therefore, the place you perform your exercises is just as crucial to happiness as the exercise itself.

When people hear the word "exercise" they automatically associate it with trying to lose weight and be healthy, which is actually a turn off for many people. But exercise is so much more than just burning fat. Exercise is actually a natural human function the same way eating and seeing are. You have to incorporate at least 20-30 minutes of exercise into your schedule each day in order to become happier. The idea for conducting any exercise routine is to try and keep your heart rate up consistently throughout the duration of your workout. If you can do this then you'll feel much happier afterwards, regardless of what kind of day you had beforehand.

Hit the outdoors. Just being in a place like this makes me happy.

As you become better at exercise, you can move on and do something else besides walking that is higher intensity. You see our bodies tend to adapt to things very easily. If you just do the same exact exercise routine every day for the same amount of time, it won't be as beneficial to your body. You need to change it up and increase the time or intensity of your exercises. In fact, the more intensity you put into your exercise the happier you will feel afterward. Just remember to consider what you are capable of doing. If you haven't exercised in a long time then don't perform a five-mile run. You have to start casually with low intensity and then work your way up to high intensity after you've trained your body. Aside from walking, you can do jogging, swimming, biking, and even weightlifting. Just experiment with different routines and have fun with it.

Using humor for happiness

There is an old saying that laughter is the best medicine for people who are sick because it makes them feel happier and takes their mind off their troubles. If you were to examine someone who is unhappy then you will find they very rarely laugh. Why do you think that is? Human beings are all capable of laughter. When we are children it is very easy to laugh because we are energetic, free, and not bombarded by the stresses that adults have to face every day. Adults are the ones who focus too much on their stresses to the point where they never want to laugh anymore. All they know how to do is feel miserable and unhappy. It even gets to a point where they are afraid of laughter because it seems so out of the norm to them. Well, if you know somebody like this then you definitely need to cheer them up with humor. It doesn't matter how many times you have to try to make them laugh. Eventually, they will come around and once they do they'll never want to go back to being a sourpuss ever again.

Smile and laugh as much as you can.

There is a famous American doctor named Hunter "Patch" Adams who is a clear example of how humor makes people happy. He is an unconventional doctor who travels the world going to developing countries where there are very sick and impoverished people. What he does is he tries to make these people laugh by dressing up like a clown or doing goofy things in front of them. Even though it isn't a cure for their problems, it does improve their quality of life and gives them something to be happy about. People in unfortunate situations if happy will have the courage and motivation to pull themselves out of whatever tough situation they are faced with. Therefore, if there were more people in the world spreading humor to others then more people would be happy as a result.

Of course, you are probably thinking about how to find humor for happiness in your own life. You could do what most people do and watch funny television sitcoms or movies. But as you have already learned in this book, watching television will make you feel depressed because you are just living vicariously through the characters on the show. Then when you turn off the television, you will feel even more depressed. So what you want to do is find humor in your real life. Hang out with a friend who is funny or go to a comedy club in your local area. You could even purchase a book of jokes and start reading them aloud or to others around you. If you are feeling confident then perhaps you could be the one at the comedy club who performs for other people and makes them laugh. Sometimes it helps to make other people laugh because then it will make you feel good about yourself. It will make you feel like you made a contribution to other people's happiness. This will do wonders for your self-esteem and self-worth.

No matter what kind of personality you have, you can laugh and make others laugh too. All you have to do is put forth the effort and develop a sense of humor. You don't have to be serious about everything in life. If you change a few difficult circumstances and find humor in them, then they won't seem so bad. That is why the people who laugh more are happier than the people who don't laugh. Wouldn't you rather be the person who laughs more? Of course, you would.

Build up self-esteem

Self-esteem is the value and respect we have for ourselves. We all grow up with different levels of self-esteem based on the experiences we've had and the people who've influenced us. If you grew up around people who belittled you and made you feel worthless, then chances are you are someone who has low self-esteem. It can take people decades after they become adults to rebuild themselves and find a way to having higher self-esteem.

I used to have low self-esteem. I started being positive and things began to change.

So what exactly builds self-esteem? The first thing you need to do is be positive about life. If you are someone who looks at the negative side of everything rather than the positive then you are going to think that you aren't capable of accomplishing anything. This will cause you to have a low opinion of yourself. Therefore, you need to turn this around by convincing yourself that you can accomplish anything with the right amount of effort. Nothing is impossible if you keep trying and working toward it. One way you can convince yourself of this is by not comparing yourself to others. You may think that comparing yourself to someone who has accomplished something will make you think you can do the same thing, but it will just end up disappointing you because you are not the same person as they are. If you are trying to reach the same success that someone else achieved in the same way then you are just going to end up failing and feeling bad about yourself. So what you need to do is stop comparing yourself to others and just let your natural abilities take over. By doing this, you will learn what your god given strengths are versus your god given weaknesses.

Now we have already touched upon 'exercise' in this book about how it makes people happier. Well, exercise can also build up your self-esteem in two different ways. The first way is the superficial way which is helping you lose weight. If we are able to make ourselves look better then we will feel better about ourselves. The second way exercise helps is by improving your mood. Once you are in a better mood, it will be much easier for you to develop a positive mindset about your life. Then you can focus more on the things you can change rather than what you can't change. People often have low self-esteem because they think about the nasty things they have dealt in life. But there are always things you can change to make your life better. Perhaps you can get a new job, move to a new location, or get out of a bad relationship. Whatever you have the power to change to make your life better, do it because you will feel better about yourself afterwards.

Most importantly, do things that you enjoy and be around supportive people. If everything you do in your life is something you don't want to do, you are going to feel like your life is pointless. The people who feel good about themselves often find time to do the activities that they want to do. That way their life will have a purpose and it will make them feel like it is a more valuable life. As for the people in your life, make sure you surround yourself with people who reinforce that your life is valuable. If you only have people who hate and criticize you, then get away from those people. There are always other groups of people out there who can be more supportive such as AA meetings, social groups, and so on. The idea is to surround yourself with more positivity and less negativity.

Eating well for happiness

Food is a very controversial thing when it comes to happiness. There are two types of foods that make people happy. There are foods that people eat for pleasure and there are foods people eat for health. The food choice that you make depends on the goals you set for yourself. If you are someone who just wants to enjoy themselves when they eat and not worry so much about the ingredients in your food, then you will have no problems with eating pizza, cookies, potato chips, and other kinds of junk foods that taste good. However, these foods will end up making you feel worse after they've had time to digest in your belly. If you care about your health then you will be happier eating healthier foods rather than processed foods.

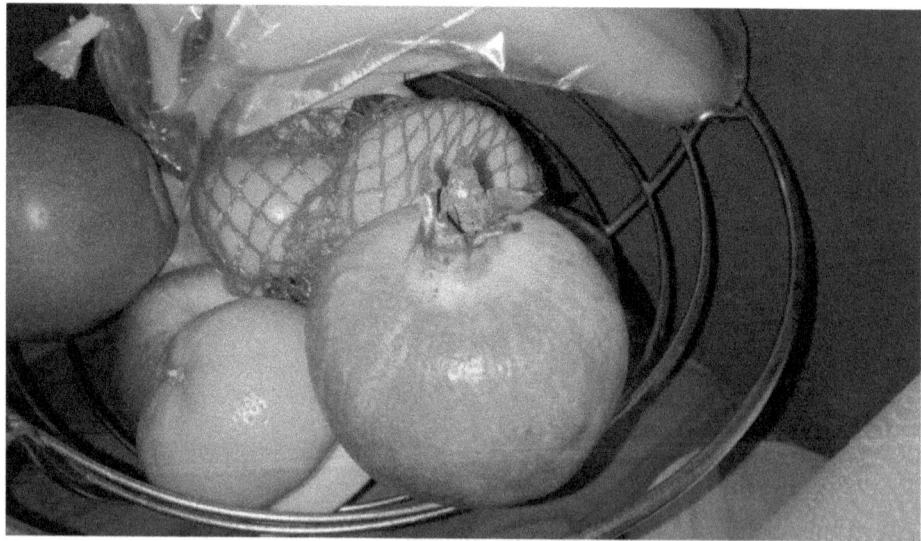

Good food for good mood. I try to have variety of fruits, full of natural goodness.

So what exactly are healthier foods? These are foods that are naturally produced by the earth rather than by human beings. Fruits and vegetables are on the top of this list because they are grown right from the ground. Although, the most critical factor of any food choice are its nutrients. These nutrients hold the key to making people feel happier and better. For example, mussels are a type of seafood that has the highest amount of vitamin B12 than any other food known to man. Vitamin B12 is known for increasing brain function and protecting it when you grow older. Mussels also have mood-regulating nutrients like selenium, zinc and iodine. If you are a seafood eater then mussels should be your top choice as a natural mood enhancer. On the other hand, if you prefer other kinds of meat then lamb is what you will want to be eating. Lamb meat contains linoleic acid which reduces brain cell inflammation and eases stress hormones of the back. It also contains iron which is great for stabilizing your mood and enhancing your concentration levels.

Glass of pomegranate juice. It's very good for you.

If you're more of a vegetable person, then try eating some blue potatoes. You'll typically find these sold at farmer's markets rather than your traditional supermarkets. The skins of blue potatoes contain antioxidants and iodine to greatly enhance your mood. Swiss chard is another mood enhancing vegetable, thanks to the magnesium in it. This is not a common vegetable that people eat, but you should be able to find it in your local grocery store. But regardless of which vegetable you purchase, try to purchase organic vegetables with no pesticides or chemical additives used. These chemical additives have been known to alter people's moods for the worst. If you have to only shop at the farmer's market then go and do it. On a side note, there are some semi-healthy foods that you can eat for a better mood. Dark chocolate is one example because it doesn't have the sugar or milk additives in it. Instead, it is just pure chocolate that has the ability to improve concentration and mood by increasing blood flow to your brain.

The strange thing about people is most of them know that fruits and vegetables are what they need to eat in order to feel better and be happier. Adults even lecture children about eating fruits and vegetables, despite adults themselves not practicing what they preach. So what is it that makes us not want to eat these healthier foods? These foods may not taste as good as junk foods, but they will make you feel good after you've eaten them. If you can remember that then it will be easier to eat healthier foods. The hardest part is taking the first step. But just remember, your happiness is on the line here! That is why it is important to follow through and eat healthily.

Talking and sharing with others for happiness

In our era of technological communication, the main way we talk to other people is through mobile texting or email over the internet. The days of socializing with people in person are becoming rarer all the time. However, talking and sharing with others online isn't the same as talking and sharing with them in person. Nature made humans as social beings which means we are supposed to interact with people face-to-face. This has a psychological effect that makes people much happier because they don't feel alone and isolated. It doesn't even matter if you like the person or people you are socializing with. For example, in most correctional facilities around the world, there is an ultimate punishment for prisoners who break the rules. This punishment is called "solitaire." This is where a prisoner is put in a room all by them self without any windows or people around. Without anyone to talk to or even see, this becomes torture for an individual. It would make someone happier just to talk to anybody rather than to talk to nobody at all. This is the power of talking to others in order to be happy.

Try to interact and talk to people.

So many people in society have trouble making friends or socializing in general because technology has cut people off from conducting in real social interactions. If you are in a situation like this then try to join social groups or go out with friends as often as possible. You could even just go to a bar by yourself and try to make new friends if you don't have anyone to go with. Also, try talking with your family more often as well. Sometimes the reason we are so unhappy is because we have cut ourselves off from the people we love the most. Then, as a result, they start to resent you for it. But if you talk to them on a regular basis then it will reinforce the love you all have for one another. This will make you a happier person when you are away from them.

Go to the bar and meet people.

As important as talking is to others, sharing is even better. If you have something that other people around you might enjoy and appreciate, then go ahead and share it with them. This will make you feel better and they will feel better as well. It doesn't even matter what you have to share. It could be a mere slice of pizza or a room in your house. The ability to share with others will improve your self-esteem because you will realize that you are a generous person who likes to do nice things for other people. To find the ultimate happiness out of talking and sharing, combine the two together. In other words, try talking to a large group of people at once and share with them the knowledge that you think will benefit them. This could be a story you tell which teaches them a life lesson or simply a lesson where they learn a new skill that will benefit their lives. As long as your lesson is free and valuable, it will make you happy to give back to people in this way.

If you are a shy person then you might find talking to people rather uncomfortable. But this uncomfortable feeling that you have goes back to your feelings of low self-esteem. If you follow the other steps in the book that talk about raising self-esteem, you will find it much easier to talk to people. Then your level of happiness will increase more without you even realizing it. So don't ever be afraid to start a conversation with someone. It could be someone at a gym, grocery store, classroom, or wherever. Every little bit of conversation goes a long way toward making you a happier person.

Thank you

Gardening makes me happy. Some cherries from my garden.

Thank you for buying this book. It means a lot to me. I hope I have been able to convince you that happiness is easy to achieve. If you eat well, hit the outdoors, do some basic exercise, bit of meditation and be positive about yourself you can be happy. If you have any questions then feel free to email or get in touch here pyt@shalusharma.com. You can visit my website and send me your messages here http://shalusharma.net

Here are some of my other books that you might wish to take a look at

amazon.com/author/shalusharma

Self Discovery Journal: 121 Thought Provoking Questions: Journal Questions for Women
Journal for Girls: 101 Thought Provoking Question: Journal Questions for Girls
Journal for Women: 105 Questions for Women with Motivational Quotes: Self Discovery Journal
Gratitude Journal: Keep a Gratitude Journal and Turn Pain to Joy
An Introduction to the Way of the Buddha: Buddhism for Beginners
Buddhist Teachings, Beliefs, Finding Enlightenment and Practicing Buddhism
Hinduism for Beginners

Thank you and God bless. Be positive be happy...